COLORADO

SEASONS

by Todd Caudle

Skyline Press

Colorado Springs, Colorado

For my wife, Barbara

*First frontispiece: Cascade below Mount Parnassus,
Arapaho National Forest*

*Second frontispiece: The Guardian and Mt. Silex
rise above Vallecito Lake, Weminuche Wilderness*

*Third frontispiece: Fall colors decorate aspen trees in
the White River National Forest*

*Facing page: Backlight on aspen leaves, Barr Trail;
Blue Columbine, Animas Forks;
Aspen leaves and dew drops, Pike National Forest;
Clearing storm over Rampart Range;
Above the trees in the Colorado State Forest*

International Standard Book Number:
ISBN 0-9632012-4-7
First printing
Photography and text by Todd Caudle
Design and layout: Todd Caudle
Editor: Jane Turnis
Copyright: © Todd Caudle, 1994
Published by Skyline Press
P.O. Box 26055
Colorado Springs, CO 80936

Printed in Hong Kong

Contents

Broken rocks and reflecting pools along the Grays Peak National Recreation Trail mirror sunset hues on McClellan Mountain

Foreword

Passion . . . this book is about passion. The passion of one man and his art. When the art form is scenic photography, many uncontrollable factors are introduced into the equation of success. Uncontrollable weather and light are both the bane and the beauty of scenic photography. A man's passion provides the continuing fuel to return again and again to capture the vision when the reality is lacking.

By the time you get to reading this foreword, you will have likely viewed most of the images in Colorado Seasons. In that first magical session you were enthralled with the scenic wonder of Colorado, except that something was different. That difference is the photographic vision of Todd Caudle.

I first met Todd when he was working the scene that ultimately became the cover of his first calendar. I was camped nearby but not shooting because of veiled overcast. When I saw his calendar cover six months later, I realized Todd's talent. That talent has grown considerably in the subsequent years.

Photo books are intended to be enjoyed forward, backward or randomly. Each image is a statement unto itself; the most successful images transport the viewer to a magical world of awe and beauty. You will find yourself repeatedly picking up Colorado Seasons and seeing Colorado through the eyes of a passionate artist. Spend some time reflecting on the moment the shutter was released. Imagine the time of day, the placement of the camera, and the temperature extremes of the moment. Note the special, fleeting moments of light.

Join Todd on his passionate journey across Colorado, and experience her wondrous seasons.

—ROGER EDRINN
Colorado photographer, author & publisher

Overleaf: A crescent moon contrasts with dusk skies over the Collegiate Peaks Wilderness

Storm clouds form over Kit Carson Peak and Willow Creek, Sangre de Cristo Wilderness

Introduction

My ancestors didn't come to Colorado in covered wagons. We arrived in a '69 Chevy Impala. My family followed my oldest brother to Colorado in 1970 after he received an appointment to the U.S. Air Force Academy near Colorado Springs.

Prior to 1970, I remember trips from suburban Chicago to Colorado to see how he was holding up under the rigors of military academy life. Once across the Kansas-Colorado border we all squinted into late-afternoon light, in hopes of being the first to spot that place where the Great Plains gave in to the majestic Colorado Rockies. The grain fields of eastern Colorado gave in to the uplifting skyline grudgingly, yet that skyline got more and more impressive with each mile westward.

When I first started pursuing photography seriously, I often cruised past some of Colorado's most beautiful scenery on my way to the red rock canyon country of southern Utah. There was something about Utah's canyons, mesas and arches that tugged at my creative senses. It was different, and far away.

Then one summer I decided to stay closer to home. I called it my "Rediscovery of Colorado." Making a commitment to explore my home state gave me a clean canvas on which to work. Something clicked - literally - and Colorado became (and remains) my favorite photo subject.

As an artist and passionate explorer, my biggest dilemma is the depth and breadth of Colorado. In a lifetime I might only scratch the surface of the state's natural wealth. Colorado is one gigantic jigsaw puzzle, each piece possessing its own unique personality. What is one man with only one lifetime to do?

For the last several years I've explored Colorado's vast treasures with much more devotion. For the rest of my life I intend to do the same. Though it's unlikely I will ever fully capture the state's beauty on film, I can hope to accomplish a lifetime of artistic and natural discovery.

The spirit of Colorado has a way of getting under your skin. For me, this place held together by four nondescript lines on a map is the very center of the universe. All my creative roads lead to the mountains, the valleys, the rivers and the plains of Colorado. The sweet scent of an alpine wildflower; the crunch of fallen aspen leaves underfoot; a shower of fine mist from a nearby waterfall; the cold snap of a pure winter sunrise. These are the things that send creative juices flowing through my veins. These are the things that shout "Colorado!"

Turn the page and explore four seasons of Mother Nature's finest work.

—TODD CAUDLE

A pine tree stands alone, Wolf Creek Pass, San Juan Mountains

Spring

Spring in its literal sense is that time between the vernal equinox and the arrival of the summer solstice. For many in America, the mere mention of spring conjures up images of cherry blossoms and tilled farm fields. Not necessarily so in Colorado. Because of the prominent mountain ranges and their elevation extremes, springtime in Colorado is like nowhere else. Instead, it's where two worlds collide. The eastern plains can be as green and fertile as a Kansas wheat field, yet at higher elevations, winter still reigns supreme. The mountains are rarely eager to shed their snowy cloak.

With all its climatic diversity, springtime in Colorado offers unending variety. At lower elevations the days are warm and the nights whisper a cool, crisp sigh. In the mountains the snow lingers, albeit in ever-diminishing patches. Alpine lakes nestle thick sheets of ice until sunny days and above-freezing nights force the ice pack's retreat. The tundra soaks up moisture from remaining snow. A trickle starts at the base of a snow drift. The trickle feeds a rivulet, and in turn teams with other tiny tributaries, building in speed and stature as it races downhill. Cutting through the alpine tundra and tumbling over rocky ledges in a series of cascades, the water courses relentlessly toward the lowlands. The landscape awakens from a long winter's sleep. Grasses sprout from the moistened land, preparing to host the annual fireworks display of alpine wildflowers that will come in July and August. A little lower, aspens begin to sprout leaves, succulent, luminescent green at first, until a heavy dose of chlorophyll turns them a darker shade.

Though the timeline of events may be more sporadic and less predictable than in many other places, it is a new beginning.

It is springtime in Colorado.

Overleaf: Fog shrouds trees in the Colorado State Forest

Rain showers saturate fresh greens in Garden of the Gods, Colorado Springs

Granite domes and reflecting pool along Goose Creek, Lost Creek Wilderness

The Maroon Bells' image resounds in a small pond reflection, White River National Forest

Spring snowmelt feeds Horseshoe Falls, Rocky Mountain National Park

Above the clouds on Rampart Range, Pike National Forest

A storm retreats from the slopes of the Grenadier Range, San Juan Mountains

Remnants of last winter's snow cling to mountainsides below Paradise Divide, Ruby Range

Evening light strikes the Nohku Crags, Colorado State Forest
Overleaf: Peaks of the Silverton West Group of the San Juan Mountains rise above the town of Silverton

Aspen trees sprout fresh leaves below Wilson Peak, San Miguel Mountains

A field of dandelions awaits afternoon showers below Wilson Peak, San Miguel Mountains

Sunset light paints peaks of the Sawatch Range, San Isabel National Forest

Summer

Even the highest alpine lakes are free of ice now. Snow can still be found in the shadows of north-facing slopes that rarely see the sun, but now the warmth of summer is transforming the snow into life-sustaining water. There's water, water everywhere, and it's soaking into the tundra, only to rise to the surface somewhere else. Small alpine lakes, or tarns, fill any depression in the landscape, where they often create stunning mirror images of their surroundings. Still more water collects in drainages that have been carved through the ages, and joins other small tributaries. The babble of tiny, tumbling brooks is Nature's symphony, and the music builds to a crescendo as the water follows gravity's course. Along the way, cascading waterfalls accent the journey, both visually and audibly.

Thanks to the moisture and the return of warmer temperatures, the short grasses and miniature flowers have awakened to enjoy the brief return of summer to the Colorado high country. Even the fragile blue columbine, Colorado's state flower, makes showy appearances in the protective shade of aspen groves and rock outcroppings. The beautiful, star-shaped flower loves such indirect light.

Although the lowlands might be basking in temperatures hovering around 85 degrees in summer months, relief is never far away. A trip to the mountains quickly transports anyone seeking a respite from the heat to a world where 70-degree days and chilly nights are the norm. Sure, you might have to dodge a few late-afternoon thunderstorms, but that's part of the fun.

Overleaf: An alpine tarn reflects symmetry below Mt. Edwards, Grays Peak National Recreation Trail

Showy daisy and shrubby cinquefoil bloom below the Three Apostles, Collegiate Peaks Wilderness

The Nohku Crags reflect afternoon light in an alpine tarn, Colorado State Forest

Marsh marigolds border an alpine pool in American Basin, San Juan Mountains

Early morning mist plays on the surface of a small lake, Collegiate Peaks Wilderness

A depression in the landscape collects late-summer snowmelt, Weminuche Wilderness

Clouds' shadows glide over granite domes in the Lost Creek Wilderness

Maroon Lake mirrors the famous Maroon Bells near Aspen

The morning sun dissipates fog in North Park, as seen from the Park Range
Overleaf: Morning alpenglow highlights peaks above Nymph Lake, Rocky Mountain National Park

Summit Lake welcomes sunrise to Buffalo Pass, Park Range

Shrubby cinquefoil enjoy their perch along a lazy stretch of Pine Creek, Collegiate Peaks Wilderness

Last light illuminates a ridge in the Sawatch Range, San Isabel National Forest

High above Lake Agnes in the Colorado State Forest, a small shelf lake reflects afternoon light

Alpine sunflowers proliferate on a hillside in Stevens Gulch, Grays Peak National Recreation Trail

Blue columbines, Colorado's state flower, show off below Grays Peak

A small pond reflects Edith Mountain, San Juan Mountains

A treeline and rock wall create a graphic pattern in the Mosquito Range
Overleaf: Blue sky reflections fill an alpine tarn below Engineer Pass, with the Sneffels Range rising in the distance

Volcanic boulders flank Nellie Creek, with Uncompahgre Peak looming overhead, Uncompahgre Wilderness

Storm clouds threaten skies above Eldorado Lake, Weminuche Wilderness

Cascades tumble over boulders below American Basin Crags, San Juan Mountains

A recent release of reservoir water swells North Clear Creek Falls, Rio Grande National Forest
Overleaf: Lower Willow Creek Lake showcases a natural symmetry in the Sangre de Cristo Wilderness

Conundrum Peak catches the first light of day, Maroon Bells-Snowmass Wilderness

The moon rises over McClellan Mountain and Stevens Creek, Grays Peak National Recreation Trail

Mosquito Creek drains the slopes of Mount Buckskin, Mosquito Range

Lush summer grasses collect water droplets from a passing storm, Emerald Lake Trail, Rocky Mountain National Park

Storm clouds build over Hayden Mountain, Yankee Boy Basin, San Juan Mountains

Broken rocks create reflecting pools on the edge of Kite Lake, San Juan Mountains

Glassy water reflects a double image of rugged Star Peak and Cooper Peak, Elk Mountains

Remnants of a deteriorating cabin stand sentinel over Difficult Creek, Collegiate Peaks Wilderness
Overleaf: Peaks of the Sawatch Range define the skyline east of Taylor Pass

Willow Creek cuts through cliffs along the eastern shore of Willow Creek Lake, Sangre de Cristo Wilderness

Sunset light brings a glow to the slopes of Mount Bross, Mosquito Range

Raindrops create ripples on Homestake Creek, White River National Forest

Holy Cross Ridge rises high above lush alpine meadows, Holy Cross Wilderness
Overleaf: Last night's mid-July snowstorm leaves its mark on Mount Harvard, Collegiate Peaks Wilderness

Snowmass Mountain dominates the view from Geneva Lake, Maroon Bells-Snowmass Wilderness

Nellie Creek rushes over rolling tundra below Uncompahgre Peak, Uncompahgre Wilderness

A shallow tarn reflects summer skies, American Flats, San Juan Mountains

Peaks of the Ruby Range rise above the town of Crested Butte
Overleaf: Towers along Castle Peak's southern ridge define a dramatic skyline, Elk Mountains

A fast-moving storm dusts Capitol Peak with early season snow, Maroon Bells-Snowmass Wilderness

Autumn

Easterners will argue that the singular hue of a changing aspen leaf can't compete with the myriad of New England's fall colors. But New England doesn't have the Rocky Mountains!

Autumn in Colorado is a scenic treasure. It is also a period of enormous transition, when desert heat waves cease and Pacific monsoonal flows diminish. Clouds change from brimstone and fire-laden cumuli to wisps of non-threatening high cirrus clouds. And the aspen forests, though not as diverse in fall colors as the oak, birch and maple forests back East, prepare for hibernation. Imperceptibly at first, a single leaf here or a branchful there, the leaves begin to show their golden hue. Leaf by leaf, tree by tree, mountainside by mountainside, waves of color ripple through the forest.

Everybody has an opinion as to when the aspens will change color, and why. It's the moisture of last winter, one will say. It's the timing of the first frost, another will counter. Sometimes it seems there are as many opinions as there are trees. Forget them all. In the blink of time's eye, Man just doesn't have a broad enough vision to predict the whimsy of nature.

Colorado autumn isn't just golden aspens quaking in the wind. Gambel oak turns crimson red. Ground cover mimics the East's rainbow of colors. But it is the changing of the aspens that is most heralded. Is it any wonder? After all, aspen trees make a conspicuous habit of growing in front of some pretty impressive backdrops. Stands of yellow create a visual foundation for the famous Maroon Bells formation near Aspen. The Sneffels Range in southwestern Colorado benefits from a similar juxtaposition. All over Colorado, aspens punctuate a landscape that hardly needs the visual aid.

Autumn in Colorado is also a time of subtleties. The musky scent of decaying aspen leaves on a forest floor. A crystalline veil of ice on the surface of an alpine tarn. The first dusting of snow on lofty peaks. The monotone color scheme of a barren aspen forest. Autumn is more than a visual time. It is a time to park the car, strap on the hiking boots and hit the trail. It is a time to hear, smell, touch and fully absorb the gifts of Nature before The Big Sleep...

Winter is on its way.

Overleaf: A barren aspen forest awaits winter, San Isabel National Forest

Grasses of the Huerfano River Valley nestle below Blanca Peak, Sangre de Cristo Wilderness

A snag mimics the triangular shape of Pyramid Peak, Maroon Bells-Snowmass Wilderness

Fallen aspen leaves provide a rich carpet for the forest floor, San Isabel National Forest

A forest floor detail reveals the annual ritual of decay, San Isabel National Forest
Overleaf: Gambel oak and golden aspens precede Mount Sneffels and the Sneffels Range, Uncompahgre National Forest

Rain saturates a rainbow of fall colors, West Maroon Creek Trail, Maroon Bells-Snowmass Wilderness

Dew drops moisten fallen aspen leaves, Pike National Forest

Colorful aspens compete for attention with Wilson Peak, San Miguel Mountains

Backlit aspens rival the beauty of the sheer ridges of Sheep Mountain, San Juan Mountains

Aspens stand straight and tall along Ragged Mountain Road, Gunnison National Forest

Dark evergreens dot a forest dominated by aspens, White River National Forest

Subtle evening light enhances fall colors below Mount Sneffels, Uncompahgre National Forest

Ranches dot the Wet Mountain Valley below the Sangre de Cristo Range
Overleaf: Chimney Rock and Courthouse Mountain turn rosy red under September light, Uncompahgre National Forest

Aspens don a variety of autumn shades below Mount Hope and Twin Peaks, San Isabel National Forest

Silhouetted aspens frame the Maroon Bells, White River National Forest

Stately cottonwood trees prepare to shed their leaves, Garden of the Gods, Colorado Springs

Eroded volcanic remnants create a unique skyline along Turret Ridge, Uncompahgre National Forest
Overleaf: Winter gets a head start in the Raggeds Wilderness

Fallen leaves accent the season's first snow, Lost Creek Wilderness

Backlight amplifies rich hues of an aspen forest, San Juan National Forest

Windswept trees frame an unnamed peak below Elkhead Pass, Collegiate Peaks Wilderness

Winter

The descriptive word for winter in Colorado is white. Snowfall defines the state, drawing skiers from around the state, the nation and the world to swoosh through knee-deep powder or break trail on backcountry ski trails.

That's not to say that Colorado is locked in an icy chill from November to April, though. Winter in many parts of Colorado is surprisingly mild. Between cold snaps, temperatures in the mid-50s and low-60s are not uncommon. Yet always, lurking in the shadow of that tree, or clinging to the north slopes of those hills over there, there's that white stuff.

Of course, in the mountains, snow is omnipresent. Snowfall debuts in early autumn on the highest peaks with a light dusting that usually melts within a few days. As alpine temperatures drop, subsequent snow stays. Each passing storm leaves its mark, creating deeper and deeper snowpack.

That annual snowpack is Colorado's liquid gold, deposited in its crystalline form in winter, and withdrawn as run-off during spring, summer and autumn. Parts of Colorado are semi-arid desert. Without run-off, much more would be. Eighty percent of Colorado's water supply is stored in mountain snows. When warmer weather loosens winter's grip, the downward flow of mountain streams supplies farmers, ranchers, city dwellers and outdoor lovers with the water so vital to their existence.

There's more to winter in Colorado than snowpack and ski parkas, though. It can be a quiet time, when a hush falls over the land and winter's breath whisks snowflakes off the ground and sends them sparkling across a cobalt blue sky. It can be a time to behold Nature's fury, too, when swirling clouds deposit several feet of snow on mountain slopes, burying the landscape in unequalled freshness - and the potential for devastating avalanches.

For so many reasons, without its winter white, Colorado wouldn't be the paradise that it is.

Overleaf: Aspen trees paint pastel shadows across virgin snow, White River National Forest

Icicles form on granite monoliths, Lost Creek Wilderness

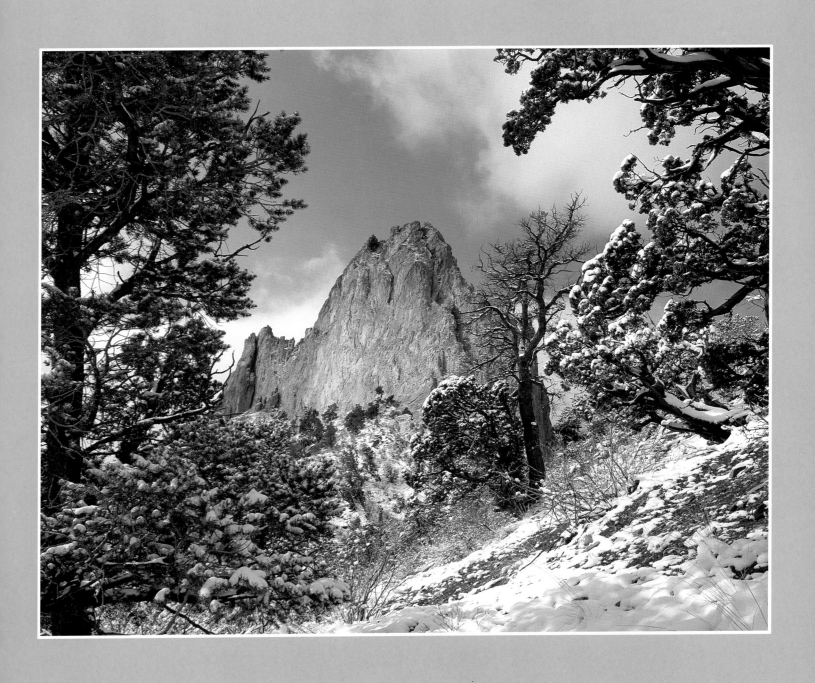

Yesterday's snowstorm creates a winter wonderland in Garden of the Gods, Colorado Springs

Rime ice clings to everything in its path at a homestead in Black Forest

Fresh snow accentuates rock textures in Roxborough State Park

The Never Summer Range captures first light in Rocky Mountain National Park

Another winter storm builds over Pikes Peak and Garden of the Gods, Colorado Springs

Longs Peak's imposing east face dominates the view along the Peak to Peak Highway near Allenspark

A patchwork of snow clings to slopes below Keyboard of the Winds, Longs Peak, Rocky Mountain National Park
Overleaf: Angular rocks of Roxborough State Park look more beautiful than ever with a fresh dusting of snow

Elongated shadows extend downhill on a mountainside in the San Juan National Forest

Patterns of light and shadow compete on the slopes of Milwaukee Peak, Sangre de Cristo Wilderness

A storm clears to reveal Sunshine Mountain, San Miguel Mountains

Another day, another clearing storm, San Miguel Mountains
Overleaf: Howling winds bond snow to aspen boles, La Veta Pass

A setting moon falls behind Kissing Camels, Garden of the Gods, Colorado Springs

Square Top Mountain defines the view west of Guanella Pass, Arapaho National Forest

Snow-capped peaks of the Never Summer Range rise high above Forest Canyon, Rocky Mountain National Park

Golden Horn and Pilot Knob tower over Ice Lakes Basin, San Juan Mountains

Wet March snow weighs heavily on pine boughs, Lizard Head Pass, San Juan Mountains

Fog shrouds clusters of aspen trees on La Veta Pass

Goose Creek meanders through Lost Creek Wilderness

Unusually heavy snowpack shrouds sand dunes under a blanket of white, Great Sand Dunes National Monument
Overleaf: Jagged peaks of the Grenadier Range dominate the view from Molas Pass, San Juan Mountains

A thick fog bank works its way up Ute Pass below Pikes Peak's rugged north face

Afternoon sun peeks through a lodgepole pine forest, Rocky Mountain National Park

A crescent moon accents predawn light in the Uncompahgre Wilderness

Timeless

Certain images of Colorado transcend seasonal description. The final chapter of
Colorado Seasons celebrates the serendipity of the magnificent Colorado landscape.

A sunset view from Wilkerson Pass reveals the outline of the Mosquito Range
Overleaf: The forest canopy reaches for the sky, San Isabel National Forest

A mountain goat enjoys its precarious perch below Mount Edwards, Grays Peak National Recreation Trail

The Gunnison River courses through Black Canyon of the Gunnison National Monument

Boulder Creek flows through a maze of weathered stones

A rising sun silhouettes Profile Rock, along the Highway of Legends Scenic Byway

One of many sandstone arches spans a gap in the crest of Rattlesnake Canyon

Great spires rise from the valley floor of the Colorado National Monument

Sand dunes rise 700 feet above the floor of San Luis Valley, Great Sand Dunes National Monument

The day's first light strikes Mount Garfield, Grand Junction's towering landmark
Overleaf: Moonrise moves over strange shapes in Garden of the Gods, Colorado Springs

151

Blackwall Mountain and Coxcomb Peak create one of Colorado's most impressive skylines, Uncompahgre National Forest

Ranching and recreation go hand in hand where the Wet Mountain Valley meets Sierra Blanca, Sangre de Cristo Range

Post-sunset light highlights a beautiful Rocky Mountain skyline west of South Park

A nearly full moon sets behind Kissing Camels, Garden of the Gods, Colorado Springs

Light and shadow yield dramatic patterns at sunset, Great Sand Dunes National Monument

The frame of an abandoned farmhouse challenges the colorful sunrise, Huerfano County

The last rays of the day fade over the Elk Mountains.
Tomorrow, mountain adventures begin again...